Tucholsky Wagner Zola Scott Sydow Freud Schlegel
Turgenev Fonatne Wallace
Twain Walther von der Vogelweide Fouqué Friedrich II. von Preußen
Weber Freiligrath Frey
Kant Ernst
Fechner Fichte Weiße Rose von Fallersleben Richthofen Frommel
Hölderlin
Engels Fielding Eichendorff Tacitus Dumas
Fehrs Faber Flaubert
Maximilian I. von Habsburg Fock Eliasberg Ebner Eschenbach
Feuerbach Eliot Zweig
Ewald Vergil
Goethe Elisabeth von Österreich London
Mendelssohn Balzac Shakespeare Dostojewski Ganghofer
Trackl Lichtenberg Rathenau Doyle Gjellerup
Stevenson Hambruch
Mommsen Tolstoi Lenz Droste-Hülshoff
Thoma von Arnim Hanrieder
Dach Verne Hägele Hauff Humboldt
Reuter Rousseau Hagen Hauptmann
Karrillon Garschin Gautier
Defoe Hebbel Baudelaire
Damaschke Descartes
Hegel Kussmaul Herder
Wolfram von Eschenbach Schopenhauer
Darwin Dickens Rilke George
Bronner Melville Grimm Jerome
Campe Horváth Aristoteles Bebel Proust
Bismarck Vigny Barlach Voltaire Federer Herodot
Gengenbach Heine
Storm Casanova Tersteegen Grillparzer Georgy
Lessing Gilm
Chamberlain Langbein Gryphius
Brentano Lafontaine
Strachwitz Claudius Schiller Kralik Iffland Sokrates
Katharina II. von Rußland Bellamy Schilling
Gerstäcker Raabe Gibbon Tschechow
Löns Hesse Hoffmann Gogol Wilde Vulpius
Luther Heym Hofmannsthal Gleim
Roth Klee Hölty Morgenstern
Heyse Klopstock Kleist Goedicke
Luxemburg Puschkin Homer
Machiavelli La Roche Horaz Mörike Musil
Navarra Aurel Musset Kierkegaard Kraft Kraus
Lamprecht Kind Hugo Moltke
Nestroy Marie de France Kirchhoff
Laotse Ipsen Liebknecht
Nietzsche Nansen
Marx Ringelnatz
von Ossietzky Lassalle Gorki Klett Leibniz
May vom Stein Lawrence
Petalozzi Irving
Platon Knigge
Sachs Pückler Michelangelo Kafka
Poe Kock
de Sade Praetorius Liebermann
Mistral Zetkin Korolenko

The publishing house tredition has created the series **TREDITION CLASSICS**. It contains classical literature works from over two thousand years. Most of these titles have been out of print and off the bookstore shelves for decades.

The book series is intended to preserve the cultural legacy and to promote the timeless works of classical literature. As a reader of a **TREDITION CLASSICS** book, the reader supports the mission to save many of the amazing works of world literature from oblivion.

The symbol of **TREDITION CLASSICS** is Johannes Gutenberg (1400 – 1468), the inventor of movable type printing.

With the series, tredition intends to make thousands of international literature classics available in printed format again – worldwide.

All books are available at book retailers worldwide in paperback and in hardcover. For more information please visit: www.tredition.com

tredition was established in 2006 by Sandra Latusseck and Soenke Schulz. Based in Hamburg, Germany, tredition offers publishing solutions to authors and publishing houses, combined with worldwide distribution of printed and digital book content. tredition is uniquely positioned to enable authors and publishing houses to create books on their own terms and without conventional manufacturing risks.

For more information please visit: www.tredition.com

Bournemouth, Poole & Christchurch

Sidney Heath

Imprint

This book is part of the TREDITION CLASSICS series.

Author: Sidney Heath
Cover design: toepferschumann, Berlin (Germany)

Publisher: tredition GmbH, Hamburg (Germany)
ISBN: 978-3-8491-4793-8

www.tredition.com
www.tredition.de

BRANKSOME CHINE, BOURNEMOUTH

One of the most picturesque of the many "chines" or openings in the coast. Branksome Chine was formerly the landing-place of the famous smuggler Gulliver, who amassed a fortune.

LIST OF ILLUSTRATIONS

The scenery which impresses most of us is certainly that in which Nature is seen in her wild and primitive condition, telling us of growth and decay, and of the land's submission to eternal laws unchecked by the hand of man. Yet we also feel a certain pleasure in the contemplation of those scenes which combine natural beauty with human artifice, and attest to the ability with which architectural science has developed Nature's virtues and concealed natural disadvantages.

To a greater extent, perhaps, than any other spot in southern England, does Bournemouth possess this rare combination of natural loveliness and architectural art, so cunningly interwoven that it is difficult to distinguish the artificial from the natural elements of the landscape.

[Pg 6]

To human agency Bournemouth owes a most delightful set of modern dwelling-houses, some charming marine drives, and an abundance of Public Gardens. Through Nature the town receives its unique group of Chines, which alone set it apart from other watering-places; its invigorating sea-breezes, and its woods of fir and pine clustering upon slopes of emerald green, and doing the town excellent service by giving warmth and colour to the landscape when winter has stripped the oak and the elm of their glowing robes.

Considerably less than a century ago Bournemouth, or "Burne-mouth", consisted merely of a collection of fishermen's huts and smugglers' cabins, scattered along the Chines and among the pine-woods. The name "Bournemouth" comes from the Anglo-Saxon words *burne*, or *bourne*, a stream, and *mûtha*, a mouth; thus the town owes its name to its situation at the mouth of a little stream which rises in the parish of Kinson some five or six miles distant.

From Kinson the stream flows placidly through a narrow valley of much beauty, and reaches the sea by way of one of those romantic Chines so characteristic of this corner of the Hampshire coast, and of the neighbouring Isle of Wight.

BOURNEMOUTH PIER AND SANDS FROM EASTCLIFF

Besides offering the usual attractions, Bournemouth Pier is the centre of a very fine system of steamship sailings to all parts of the coast.

A century ago the whole of the district between [Pg 7] Poole on the west and Christchurch on the east was an unpeopled waste of pine and heather, and the haunt of gangs of smugglers. So great had the practice of smuggling grown in the eighteenth century, that, in 1720, the inhabitants of Poole presented to the House of Commons a petition, calling attention to "the great decay of their home manufacturers by reason of the great quantities of goods run, and prayed the House to provide a remedy". In 1747 there flourished at Poole a notorious band of smugglers known as the "Hawkhurst Gang", and towards the close of the same century a famous smuggler named Gulliver had a favourite landing-place for his cargoes at Branksome Chine, whence his pack-horses made their way through the New Forest to London and the Midlands, or travelled westward across Crichel Down to Blandford, Bath, and Bristol.

Gulliver is said to have employed fifty men, who wore a livery, powdered hair, and smock frocks. This smuggler amassed a large fortune, and he had the audacity to purchase a portion of Eggardon Hill, in west Dorset, on which he planted trees to form a mark for his homeward-bound vessels. He also kept a band of watchmen in readiness to light a beacon fire on the approach of danger. This state of things continued until an Act of Parliament was passed [Pg 8] which made the lighting of signal fires by unauthorized persons a punishable offence. The Earl of Malmesbury, in his *Memoirs of an Ex-Minister*, relates many anecdotes and adventures of Gulliver, who lived to a ripe old age without molestation by the authorities, for the reason, it is said, that during the wars with France he was able to obtain, through his agents in that country, valuable information of the movement of troops, with the result that his smuggling was allowed to continue as payment for the services he rendered in disclosing to the English Government the nature of the French naval and military plans.

Warner, writing about 1800, relates that he saw twenty or thirty wagons, laden with kegs, guarded by two or three hundred horse-men, each bearing three tubs, coming over Hengistbury Head, and making their way in the open day past Christchurch to the New Forest.

On a tombstone at Kinson we may read: —

> "A little tea, one leaf I did not steal;
> For guiltless blood shed I to God appeal;
> Put tea in one scale, human blood in t'other,
> And think what 'tis to slay thy harmless brother".

The villagers of Kinson are stated to have all been smugglers, and to have followed no other occupation, while it is said that certain deep [Pg 9] markings on the walls of the church tower were caused by the constant rubbing of the ropes used to draw up and lower the kegs of brandy and the cases of tea.

That many church towers in the neighbourhood were used for the storage of illicit cargoes is well known, and the sympathies of the local clergy were nearly always on the side of the smugglers in the days when a keg of old brandy would be a very acceptable present in a retired country parsonage. Occasionally, perhaps, the parson took more than a passive interest in the proceedings. A story still circulates around the neighbourhood of Poole to the effect that a new-comer to the district was positively shocked at the amount of smuggling that went on. One night he came across a band of smug-glers in the act of unloading a cargo. "Smuggling," he shouted. "Oh, the sin of it! the shame of it! Is there no magistrate, no justice of the peace, no clergyman, no minister, no — —"

"There be the Parson," replied one of the smugglers, thinking it was a case of sickness.

"Where? Where is he?" demanded the stranger.

"Why, that's him a-holding of the lanthorn," was the laconic reply.

It was early in the nineteenth century that a Mr. Tregonwell of Cranborne, a Dorset man who owned [Pg 10] a large piece of the moorland, found, on the west side of the Bourne Valley, a sheltered combe of exceptional beauty, where he built a summer residence (now the Exeter Park Hotel), the first real house to be erected on the virgin soil of Bournemouth. A little later the same gentleman also built some cottages, and the "Tregonwell Arms", an inn which became known as the half-way house between Poole and Christchurch, and so remained until it was pulled down to make way for other buildings.

These, however, were isolated dwellings, and it was not until 1836 that Sir George Gervis, Bart., of Hinton Admiral, Christchurch, commenced to build on an extensive scale on the eastern side of the stream, and so laid the foundations of the present town. Sir George employed skilful engineers and eminent architects to plan and lay out his estate, so that from the beginning great care was taken in the formation and the selection of sites for the houses and other buildings, with the result that Bournemouth is known far and wide as the most charming, artistic, and picturesque health resort in the country. This happy result is due, in a large measure, to the care with which its natural features have been preserved and made to harmonize with the requirements of a large residential population. It is equally gratifying to note that successive [Pg 11] landowners, and the town's Corporation, following the excellent example set by Sir George Gervis, continue to show a true conservative instinct in preserving all that is worthy of preservation, while ever keeping a watchful eye on any change which might detract from the unique beauty of Bournemouth.

BOURNEMOUTH: THE SQUARE AND GARDEN FROM MONT DORE

The town is situated on the curve of a large and open bay, bounded by lofty if not precipitous cliffs, which extend as far west as Haven Point, the entrance to Poole Harbour, and eastwards to Hengistbury Head, a distance of fourteen miles from point to point.

In addition to its splendid marine drives, its retiring vales, its pine-woods, and its rustic nooks and dells, the town is splendidly provided with Public Gardens, excellently laid out, and luxuriously planted in what was once mere bog and marsh land. The Gardens contain a liberal supply of choice evergreens, and deciduous shrubs and trees, while it is noticeable that the *Ceanothus azureus* grows here without requiring any protection. The slopes of the Gardens rise gradually to where the open downs are covered with heaths, gorse, and plantations of pines and firs.

It was not long after the first houses had been built that the true source of Bournemouth's attractiveness was realized to be her climate, her salt-laden breezes, and her pine-scented air. Since then she has become more and more sought, both for residential [Pg 12] and visiting purposes. Year by year the town has spread and broadened, stretching out wide arms to adjacent coigns of vantage like Parkstone, Boscombe, Pokesdown, and Southbourne, until the "Queen of the South" now covers many miles in extent.

It is one of those favoured spots where Autumn lingers on till Christmas, and when Winter comes he is Autumn's twin brother, only distinguishable from him by an occasional burst of temper, in the form of an east wind, soon repented of and as soon forgotten. Thus it is that a large number of holiday visitors are tempted to make their stay a long one, and every winter brings an increasingly greater number of new-comers to fill the places of the summer absentees, so that, taking the year through, Bournemouth is always full.

Contrast is one of the charms of the place; contrast between the shade and quietude of the pine-woods, and the whirl and movement of modern life and luxury in its most splendid and pronounced development.

It is a town whose charm and whose reproach alike is its newness; but unlike many an ancient town, it has no unlovely past to rise up and shame it. The dazzle and glitter of the luxury which has descended upon her wooded shores does not frighten Bournemouth, since she was born in splendour, and [Pg 13] the very brightness of her short life is compensation enough for the lack of an historical, and perhaps a melancholy past.

With the exception of the soil on which she stands, and the growths of that soil, everything in Bournemouth is modern—churches, houses, and shops—but all are as beautiful as modern architects and an unlimited supply of money can make them. There are hundreds of costly houses, charming both within and without; their gardens always attractive in the freshness of their flowers, and in the trimness of their tree-lined lawns. On every side there is evidence of a universal love and culture of flowers, due, no doubt, to the wonderful climate. Nowhere are geraniums larger or redder, roses fairer or sweeter, or foliage beds more magnificently laid out; while in few other parts of the country can one find so many large houses, representative of the various schools of modern architectural art, as in Bournemouth and her tree-clad parks.

Another factor that has played a large part in the rapid development of the town is the excellence of the railway services from all parts of the country, and particularly from London. During the summer months several trains run daily from Waterloo to Bournemouth without a stop, doing the journey in two hours; so that if the London and South Western [Pg 14] Railway Company are fortunate in having a monopoly of this traffic, the town is equally fortunate in being served by a railway company which has made it almost a marine suburb of London.

Bournemouth West Railway Station, situated on Poole Hill, was completed and the line opened in the summer of 1874. In 1884-5 the Central Station, or Bournemouth East as it was then called, was built, and the two stations connected by a loop-line.

The whole of the Bournemouth district lies in the western part of the great valley or depression which stretches from Shoreham, in

Sussex, to near Dorchester, occupying the whole of South Hampshire and the greater part of the south of Sussex and Dorset. The valley is known as the chalk basin of Hampshire, and is formed by the high range of hills extending from Beachy Head to Cerne Abbas. To the north the chain of hills remains intact, whilst the southern portion of the valley has been encroached upon, and two great portions of the wall of chalk having been removed, one to the east and one to the west, the Isle of Wight stands isolated and acts as a kind of breakwater to the extensive bays, channels, and harbours which have been scooped out of the softer strata by the action of the sea. Sheltered by the Isle of Wight are the Solent and Southampton Water; westward are the bays and harbours of [Pg 15] Christchurch, Bournemouth, Poole, Studland, and Swanage. The great bay between the promontories of the Needles and Ballard Down, near Swanage, is subdivided by the headland of Hengistbury Head into the smaller bays of Christchurch and Bournemouth.

THE WINTER GARDENS, BOURNEMOUTH

The famous Winter Gardens and spacious glass Pavilion where concerts are held are under the management of the Corporation. Bournemouth spends a sum of £6000 annually in providing band music for her visitors.

The site of the town is an elevated tableland formed by an extensive development of Bagshot sands and clays covered with peat or turf, and partly, on the upland levels, with a deep bed of gravel.

The sea-board is marked with narrow ravines, gorges, or glens, here called "Chines", but in the north of England designated "Denes".

For boating people the bay affords a daily delight, although Christchurch and Poole are the nearest real harbours. At the close of a summer's day, when sea and sky and shore are enveloped in soft mist, nothing can be more delightful than to flit with a favouring wind past the picturesque Chines, or by the white cliffs of Studland. The water in the little inlets and bays lies still and blue, but out in the dancing swirl of waters set up by the sunken rocks at the base of a headland, all the colours of the rainbow seem to be running a race together. Yachts come sailing in from Cowes, proud, beautiful shapes, their polished brass-work glinting in the sunlight, while farther out in the Channel a great ocean liner steams [Pg 16] steadily towards the Solent, altering her course repeatedly as she nears the Needles.

And yet, with all her desirable qualities and attractive features, Bournemouth is not to everyone's taste, particularly those whose holidays are incomplete without mediæval ruins on their doorsteps. The town, however, is somewhat fortunate even in this respect, since, although she has no antiquities of her own, she is placed close to Wimborne and Poole on the one hand, and to Christchurch, with its ancient Priory, on the other. Poole itself is not an ideal place to live in, while Wimborne and Christchurch are out-of-the-way spots, interesting enough to the antiquary, but dull, old-fashioned towns for holiday makers. The clean, firm sands of Bournemouth are excellent for walking on, and make it possible for the pedestrian to tramp, with favourable tides, the whole of the fourteen miles of shore that separate Poole Harbour from Christchurch. By a coast ramble of this kind the bold and varied forms of the cliffs, and the coves cutting into them, give an endless variety to the scene; while many a pretty peep may be obtained where the Chines open out to the land, or where the warmly-coloured cliffs glow in the sunlight between the deep blue of the sea and the sombre tints of the heather lands and the pine-clad moor beyond.

The clays and sandy beds of these cliffs are [Pg 17] remarkable for the richness of their fossil flora. From the white, grey, and brownish clays between Poole Harbour and Bournemouth, no fewer than nineteen species of ferns have been determined. The west side of Bournemouth is rich in Polypodiaceæ, and the east side in Eucalypti and Araucaria. These, together with other and sub-tropical forms, demonstrate the existence of a once luxuriant forest that extended to the Isle of Wight, where, in the cliffs bounding Alum Bay, are contemporaneous beds. The Bournemouth clay beds belong to the Middle Eocene period.

Westwards from the Pier the cliffs are imposing, on one of the highest points near the town being the Lookout. A hundred yards or so farther on is Little Durley Chine, beyond which is a considerable ravine known as Great Durley Chine, approached from the shore by Durley Cove. The larger combe consists of slopes of sand and gravel, with soft sand hummocks at the base; while on the western side and plateau is a mass of heather and gorse. Beyond Great Durley Chine is Alum Chine, the largest opening on this line of coast. Camden refers to it as "Alom Chine Copperas House".

The views from the plateaux between the Chines are very beautiful, especially perhaps that from Branksome Chine, where a large portion of the Branksome Tower estate seems to be completely isolated by [Pg 18] the deep gorges of the Chine. This estate extends for a considerable distance to where a Martello tower, said to have been built with stones from Beaulieu Abbey, stands on the cliff, from which point the land gradually diminishes in height until, towards the entrance to Poole Harbour, it becomes a jumbled and confused mass of low and broken sand-hills. These North Haven sand-hills occupy a spit of land forming the enclosing arm of the estuary on this side. Near Poole Head the bank is low and narrow; farther on it expands until, at the termination of North Haven Point, it is one-third of a mile broad. Here the sand-dunes rise in circular ridges, resembling craters, many reaching a height of fifty or sixty feet. Turning Haven Point, the view of the great sheet of water studded with green islands and backed by the purple hills of Dorset is one of the finest in England. From Haven Point one may reach Poole along a good road that skirts the shores of the harbour all the way, and affords some lovely vistas of shimmering water and pine-clad banks.

Poole Harbour looks delightful from Haven Point. At the edge of Brownsea Island the foam-flecked beach glistens in the sun. The sand-dunes fringing the enclosing sheet of water are yellow, the salt-marshes of the shallow pools stretch in surfaces [Pg 19] of dull umber, brightened in parts by vivid splashes of green. On a calm day the stillness of utter peace seems to rest over the spot, broken only by the lapping of the waves, and the hoarse cries of the sea-birds as they search for food on the mud-banks left by the receding tide. With such a scene before us it is difficult to realize that only a mile or two distant is one of the most popular watering-places in England, with a throng of fashionable people seeking their pleasure and their health by the sea.

IN THE UPPER GARDENS, BOURNEMOUTH

These Gardens are contained within the Branksome estate, and are consequently thrown open to visitors only by the courtesy of the owner.

It is well worth while to take a boat and pull over to Brownsea. The island, which once belonged to Cerne Abbey, is elliptical in shape, with pine-covered banks rising, in some places, to a height of ninety feet. In the centre of the isle is a valley in which are two ornamental lakes. In addition to a large residence, Brownsea Castle, and its extensive grounds, there is a village of about twenty cottages, called Maryland, and an ornate Gothic church, partly roofed and panelled with fine old oak taken from the Council Chamber of Crossby Hall, Cardinal Wolsey's palace. The island once had a hermit occupier whose cell and chapel were dedicated to St. Andrew, and when Canute ravaged the Frome Valley early in the eleventh century he carried his spoils to Brownsea. The Castle was first built by Henry VIII for the protection of the harbour, on [Pg 20] condition that the town of Poole supplied six men to keep watch and ward. In 1543 the Castle was granted to John Vere, Earl of Oxford, who sold it to John Duke. In the reign of Elizabeth it was termed "The Queen's Majestie's Castell at Brownecksea", and in 1576 the Queen sold it, together with Corfe Castle, to Sir Christopher Hatton, whom she made "Admiral of Purbeck". In the early days of the Great Rebellion the island was fortified for the Parliament, and, like Poole, it withstood the attacks of the Royalists. In 1665, when the Court was at Salisbury, an outbreak of the plague sent Charles II and a few of his courtiers on a tour through East Dorset. On 15th September of that year Poole was visited by a distinguished company, which included the King, Lords Ashley, Lauderdale, and Arlington, and the youthful Duke of Monmouth, whose handsome face and graceful bearing were long remembered in the town. After the royal party had been entertained by Peter Hall, Mayor of Poole, they went by boat to Brownsea, where the King "took an exact view of the said Island, Castle, Bay, and Harbour to his great contentment".

Little could the boyish Duke of Monmouth have then foreseen that fatal day, twenty years later, when he crossed the road from Salisbury again like a hunted animal in his vain endeavour to reach the shelter of [Pg 21] the New Forest; and still less, perhaps, could his father have foreseen that Antony Etricke, whom he had made Recorder of Poole, would be the man before whom his hapless son was taken to be identified before being sent to London, and the Tower.

The next owner of Brownsea was a Mr. Benson, who succeeded Sir Christopher Wren as first surveyor of works. When he bought the island, he began to alter the old castle and make it into a residence. The burgesses of Poole claimed that the castle was a national defence, of which they were the hereditary custodians. Mr. Benson replied that as he had paid £300 for the entire island the castle was naturally included. In 1720 the town authorities appealed to George II, and in 1723 Mr. Benson and his counsel appeared before the Attorney-general, when the proceedings were adjourned, and never resumed, so that the purchaser appears to have obtained a grant of the castle from the Crown. Mr. Benson was an enthusiastic botanist and he planted the island with various kinds of trees and shrubs. He also made a collection of the many specimens of plants growing on the island.

During the next hundred and thirty years Brownsea had various owners, including Colonel Waugh (notorious for his connection with the disastrous failure of the British Bank) and the Right Hon. Frederick [Pg 22] Cavendish Bentinck, who restored the castle and imported many beautiful specimens of Italian sculpture and works of art. At the end of 1900 the estate was bought by Mr. Charles Van Raalte, to whose widow it still belongs.

Shortly before his death Mr. Van Raalte wrote a brief account of his island home, which closed with the following lines:—

> "All through the island the slopes are covered
> with rhododendrons, juniper, Scotch firs, insignis,
> macrocarpa, Corsican pines, and many other varie-
> ties of evergreens, plentifully mingled with cedars
> and deciduous forest trees. Wild fowl in great va-
> riety visit the island, and the low-lying land within

the sea-wall is the favourite haunt of many sea-birds; and several varieties of plover, the redshank, greenshank, sandpiper, and snipe may be found there. The crossbill comes very often, and the green woodpecker's cry is quite familiar. But perhaps the most beautiful little winged creature that favours us is the kingfisher."

A prominent feature on the mainland as seen from Brownsea is the little Early English church of Arne, standing on a promontory running out into the mud-banks of the estuary, and terminating in a narrow tongue of land known as Pachin's Point. At one time Arne belonged to the Abbey of Shaftesbury, and it is said that the tenants of the estate, on paying their rent, were given a ticket entitling them to a free dinner at the Abbey when they were passing through Shaftesbury. The vast [Pg 23] size of Poole Harbour is realized when we consider that, excluding the islands, its extent is ten thousand acres, and from no other spot does the sheet of water look more imposing than from the wooded heights and sandy shores of Brownsea. At low tide several channels can be traced by the darker hue of the water as it winds between the oozy mud-banks, but at high tide the whole surface is flooded, and there lies the great salt lake with her green islands set like emerald gems on a silver targe.

Eastwards from Bournemouth Pier the cliffs are bold and lofty, and are broken only by small chines or narrow gullies. On the summit of the cliff a delightful drive has been constructed, while an undercliff drive, extending for a mile and a half between Bournemouth Pier and Boscombe Pier, was formally opened with great festivities on 3rd June, 1914. Boscombe Chine, the only large opening on the eastern side of Bournemouth, must have been formerly rich in minerals, and Camden, who calls it "Bascombe", tells us that it had a "copperas house". On the eastern side of the Chine a spring has been enclosed, the water being similar to the natural mineral water of Harrogate. The whole of the Chine has been laid out as a pleasure garden, although care has been taken to preserve much of its natural wildness. Unlike most of the other chines along this stretch of shore, the [Pg 24] landward termination of Boscombe Chine is very abrupt, which is the more remarkable as the little stream by which it is watered occupies only a very slight depression beyond the Christchurch road on its way down to the sea from Littledown Heath. Boscombe House stood formerly in the midst of a fine wood of Scotch pines. The estate is now being rapidly developed for residential purposes. The house was the home for many years of descendants of the poet Shelley, who erected a monument in Christchurch Priory to the memory of their illustrious ancestor. The house lies between the Christchurch road and the sea, and was almost entirely rebuilt by Sir Percy Shelley about the middle of the nineteenth century. The rapid growth of Boscombe may be gauged by the fact that between thirty and forty years ago Boscombe House and a few primitive cottages were the only buildings between Bournemouth and Pokesdown. Like her parent of Bournemouth, whom she closely resembles, Boscombe is built on what was once a stretch of sandy heaths and pine-woods. A pier was opened here in 1889 by the Duke of Argyll. It was built entirely by private enterprise, and it was not until 1904 that it was taken over by the Corporation. To the east of the pier the cliffs have been laid out as gardens, much of the land having been given by the owners of Boscombe House on their succeeding [Pg 25] to the estate. The roads here are very similar to those of Bournemouth, with their rows of pines, and villas encircled by the same beautiful trees. A peculiar designation of Owl's Road has no direct connection with birds, but is commemorative of *The Owl*, a satirical journal in which Sir Henry Drummond Wolfe, a large landowner of Boscombe, was greatly interested.

BOSCOMBE CHINE

From Boscombe Pier very pleasant walks can be taken along the sands or on the cliffs. From the sands a long slope leads up to Fisherman's Walk, a beautiful pine-shaded road, although houses are now being built and so somewhat despoiling the original beauty of the spot. The cliffs may be regained once more at Southbourne, and after walking for a short distance towards Hengistbury Head the road runs inland to Wick Ferry, where the Stour can be crossed and a visit paid to the fine old Priory of Christchurch. Wick Ferry is one of the most beautiful spots in the neighbourhood, and is much resorted to by those who are fond of boating. Large and commodious ferry-boats land passengers on the opposite bank within a few minutes' walk of Christchurch. The main road from Bournemouth to Christchurch crosses the Stour a short distance inland from Wick Ferry by Tuckton Bridge with its toll-house, a reminder that, by some old rights, toll is still levied on all those who [Pg 26] cross the Stour, whether they use the bridge or the ferry.

Bournemouth is very proud of her Public Gardens, as she has every right to be. Out of a total area of nearly 6000 acres no fewer than 694 acres have been laid out as parks and pleasure grounds. The Pleasure Gardens are divided by the Square, that central meeting-place of the town's tramway system, into two portions, known as the Lower and the Upper Gardens. These follow the course of the Bourne stream, and they have had a considerable influence in the planning of this portion of the town. The Pinetum is the name given to a pine-shaded avenue that leads from the Pier to the Arcade Gate. Here, in storm or shine, is shelter from the winter wind or shade from the summer sun, while underfoot the fallen acicular leaves of the pines are impervious to the damp. These Gardens are more than a mile and a half in extent, and are computed to possess some four miles of footpaths. The Upper Gardens are contained within the Branksome estate, and are consequently thrown open to the public only by the courtesy of the owner. They extend to the Coy Pond, and are much quieter and less thronged with people than the Lower Gardens, with their proximity to the Pier and the shore.

Another of those picturesque open spaces which [Pg 27] do so much to beautify the town is Meyrick Park, opened in 1894, and comprising some hundred and twenty acres of undulating land on which an eighteen-hole golf course has been constructed. Another course of a highly sporting character is in Queen's Park, reached by way of the Holdenhurst Road. Beyond the Meyrick Park Golf Links lie the Talbot Woods, a wide extent of pine forest which may fittingly be included in Bournemouth's parks. These woods are the property of the Earl of Leven and Melville, who has laid down certain restrictions which must be observed by all visitors. Bicycles are allowed on the road running through the woods, but no motor cars or dogs, and smoking is rightly forbidden, as a lighted match carelessly thrown among the dry bracken with which the woods are carpeted would cause a conflagration appalling to contemplate.

The famous Winter Gardens are under the management of the Corporation, and in 1893 the spacious glass Pavilion was taken over by the same authority. It may be mentioned incidentally that Bournemouth spends a sum of six thousand pounds annually in providing band music for her visitors. The full band numbers no fewer than fifty musicians, and is divided into two portions, one for the Pier, the other for the Pavilion. The Winter Gardens are charmingly laid out with shrubs and ornamental flower beds, and on [Pg 28] special gala days clusters of fairy lights give an added brilliancy to the scene.

Boscombe possesses her own group of gardens and open spaces. Boscombe Chine Gardens extend from the Christchurch Road to the mouth of the Chine. At the shore end is an artificial pond where the juvenile natives meet the youthful visitors for the purpose of sailing toy ships. The Knyveton Gardens lie in the valley between Southcote Road and Knyveton Road, and cover some five acres of land. King's Park, and the larger Queen's Park, together with Carnarvon Crescent Gardens, show that Boscombe attaches as much importance as Bournemouth to the advantages of providing her visitors and residents with an abundance of open spaces, tastefully laid out, and having, in some cases, tennis courts and bowling greens.

The piers of both Bournemouth and Boscombe are great centres of attraction for visitors, apart from those who only use them for the purpose of reaching the many steamboats that ply up and down the coast. A landing pier of wood, eight hundred feet long and sixteen feet in width, was opened on 17th September, 1861. It cost the modest sum of £4000. During the winter of 1865-6 many of the wooden piles were found to have rotted, and were replaced by iron piles. A considerable portion of the pier was treated in a similar manner in 1866, and again in 1868. With this [Pg 29] composite and unsightly structure Bournemouth was content until 1878, when the present pier was commenced, being formally opened in 1880. It was extended in 1894, and again in 1909. Boscombe Pier, as already stated, was opened in 1889 by the then Duke of Argyll.

BOURNEMOUTH: THE CHILDREN'S CORNER, LOWER GARDENS

Owing to their proximity to the Pier and the shore, these Gardens are much frequented by the people and afford great delight to children.

Of Bournemouth's many modern churches that of St. Peter, situated at the junction of the Gervis and the Hinton Roads, has interesting historical associations, apart from its architectural appeal.

In the south transept John Keble used to sit during his prolonged stay at Bournemouth in the closing years of his life. He is commemorated by the "Keble Windows", and the "Keble Chapel", within the church, and by a metal tablet affixed to the house "Brookside", near the pier, where he passed away in 1866. The churchyard is extremely pretty, being situated on a well-wooded hillside. The churchyard cross was put up in July, 1871. In the churchyard are buried the widow of the poet Shelley, together with her father, Godwin the novelist, and her mother, who was also a writer of some distinction. Taken altogether, this church, with its splendid windows and richly-wrought reredos and screens, is one of the most pleasing modern churches in the country, both with regard to its architecture and its delightful situation.

This hillside churchyard under the pine trees, [Pg 30] together with "Brookside", where Keble lived, and Boscombe Manor, with its memories of the Shelleys, are the only literary shrines Bournemouth as yet possesses.

Mary Godwin, whose maiden name was Wollstonecraft, was an Irish girl who became literary adviser to Johnson, the publisher, by whom she was introduced to many literary people, including William Godwin, whom she married in 1797. Their daughter Mary, whose birth she did not survive, became the poet Shelley's second wife. Mary Wollstonecraft Shelley was one of the earliest writers on woman's suffrage, and her *Vindications of the Rights of Women* was much criticized on account of, to that age, the advanced views it advocated. Among her other books was a volume of *Original Stories for Children*, illustrated by William Blake.

Her father, William Godwin, was a native of Wisbeach, where he was born in 1756, and at first he was ordained for the Presbyterian ministry. He was the author of a good many novels and philosophical works. In the later years of his life he was given the office of "Yeoman Usher of the Exchequer".

It was Mary Godwin with whom Shelley eloped to Italy in 1814, and whom he married in 1816, on the death of his first wife, Harriet Westbrook, who drowned herself. In 1851, Mary Shelley was laid by the side [Pg 31] of her father and mother, brought down from St. Pancras Churchyard, and her own son, and the woman who was loved by that son, all now sleep their last sleep under the greensward of St. Peter's Church. To many of us it is the one spot in Bournemouth most worth visiting. Climbing the wooded hill we stand by the Shelley grave, and think of how much intellect, aspiration, and achievement lies there entombed, and of the pathetic cenotaph to the memory of the greatest of all the Shelleys in the fine old Priory of Christchurch, five miles away.

Previous to his coming to Bournemouth to recover his health, John Keble was vicar of Hursley, near Winchester. *The Christian Year*, upon which his literary position must mainly rest, was published anonymously in 1827. It met with a remarkable reception, and its author becoming known, Keble was appointed to the Chair of Poetry at Oxford, which he held until 1841. In the words of a modern writer, "Keble was one of the most saintly and unselfish men who ever adorned the Church of England, and, though personally shy and retiring, exercised a vast spiritual influence upon his generation". His "Life" was written by J. D. Coleridge in 1869, and again, by the Rev. W. Lock, in 1895.

The Stour valley, with its picturesque river scenery, forms a charming contrast to the seaboard of [Pg 32] Bournemouth and her suburbs of Boscombe and Southborne, while to those who are fond of river boating the whole district is full of attraction. For the pedestrian the valley is very accessible. The route from Bournemouth is by way of the Upper Gardens, and right through the Talbot Woods to Throop, where the banks of the river are covered with trees. The village is a straggling one, and the mill and weir give an additional charm to some of the prettiest river scenery in the neighbourhood. A short distance from Throop is the village of Holdenhurst, which, with Throop, forms one parish.

While in this district a visit may be paid to Hurn, or Heron Court, the seat of the Earl of Malmesbury. The house, largely rebuilt since it was owned by the Priors of Christchurch, is not shown to the public, but the park, with its beautiful plantation of rhododendrons, may be seen from the middle of May till the end of June, that is, when the flowers are in full bloom. From Holdenhurst the return journey may be made by way of Iford, and so on to the main road at Pokesdown, whence Bournemouth is soon reached.

TALBOT WOODS, BOURNEMOUTH

To those who visit the ancient town of Poole for the first time by road from Bournemouth, it is difficult to tell where the one town ends and the other begins, so continuous are the houses, shops, [Pg 33] and other buildings which line each side of the main thoroughfare; and this notwithstanding that to the left hand of the road connecting the two places lies the charming residential district of Parkstone, where the houses on a pine-clad slope look right over the great harbour of Poole. As a matter of fact Bournemouth is left long before Parkstone is reached. The County Gates not only mark the municipal boundaries of Bournemouth, but they indicate also, as their title implies, that they divide the counties of Hampshire and Dorset. Thus it is that although the beautiful houses of Branksome and Parkstone are linked to those of Bournemouth by bricks and mortar, as well as by road, rail, and tramway, they otherwise form no part of it. They are in Dorset, and county rivalry is never stronger or keener than where two beautiful residential districts face each other from opposite sides of a boundary line. Bournemouth would dearly like to take Parkstone, a natural offshoot from herself, under her municipal care, but if this were done Dorset would lose some of her most valuable rateable property, as, between them, Poole and Parkstone pay no less than one-fifth of the whole of the county rate of Dorset.

Just beyond Parkstone a lovely view is obtained of Poole Harbour from the summit of Constitution Hill.

[Pg 34]

Poole and Hamworthy, with their many industries and busy wharves, form a piquant contrast to spick-and-span Bournemouth with her tidy gardens and well-dressed crowds; but whatever the port of Poole may lack in other ways she has an abundance of history, although her claim to figure as a Roman station has been much disputed. We do know, however, that after the Norman Conquest Poole was included in the neighbouring manor of Canford, and its first charter was granted by William Longspée, Earl of Salisbury. It was not until the reign of the third Edward that the town became of much importance. This monarch used it as a base for fitting out his ships during the protracted war with France, and in 1347 it furnished and manned four ships for the siege of Calais. The lands that lie between Poole and Hamworthy were held in the Middle Ages by the Turbervilles, of Bere Regis, and during the Stuart period by the Carews, of Devonshire. In the reign of Queen Elizabeth the town had a considerable commerce with Spain until the war with that country put a stop to this particular traffic. As some compensation for their losses in this direction Elizabeth granted the town two new charters, and confirmed all its ancient privileges. During the Great Rebellion the town was held for the Parliament, and in 1642 the Royalist forces, [Pg 35] under the leadership of the Marquis of Hertford, attempted its capture, but were forced to retreat.

The town is situated on a peninsula on the north side of Poole Harbour, and at one time it was the home of many smugglers. Part of an old smuggler's house has recently been discovered in the town.

The quayside is always a busy spot, and a good deal of shipbuilding and repairing is still carried on. The town is full of old houses, although many of them are hidden behind modern fronts.

In 1885 the late Lord Wimborne presented the Corporation with some forty acres of land to be converted into a Public Park. This land has been carefully laid out, and includes tennis courts and a spacious cricket ground.

As a seaport the town was of great importance and the Royalists spared no efforts to effect its capture, but like the other Dorset port of Lyme Regis, so gallantly defended by Robert Blake, afterwards the famous admiral, Poole held out to the end. Clarendon, the Royalist historian of the Great Rebellion, makes a slighting reference to the two towns. "In Dorsetshire", he says, "the enemy had only two little fisher towns, Poole and Lyme." The "little fisher towns", however, proved a thorn in the sides of the Royalists, some thousands of whom lost [Pg 36] their lives in the fierce fighting that took place at Poole, and particularly around Lyme Regis.

The merchants of Poole became wealthy by their trade with Newfoundland, a commerce that commenced in the reign of Queen Elizabeth, and lasted until well on in the reign of Queen Victoria. The trade is said to have been conducted on the truck system, and the merchants grew rich by buying both their exports and imports wholesale while disposing of them at retail prices.

Not far from the quay is an almshouse, built in 1816 by George Garland, a wealthy merchant of the town, who, on the occasion of a great feast in 1814, presented "one honest plum-pudding of one hundredweight" towards the entertainment. Farther on is a house built in 1746 by Sir Peter Thompson. It is a good specimen of Georgian architecture, and still bears the heraldic arms of the merchant who built it. Sir Peter's house is now Lady Wimborne's "Cornelia Hospital". Most of the other old houses of the town's merchants have been modernized and sadly disfigured. The oldest almshouses—and the number of ancient almshouses in a town is a sure guide to its old-time prosperity—were built originally in the reign of the fifth Henry, and for many years belonged to the Guild of St. George. In 1547, at the Reformation, they passed to the Crown, with [Pg 37] all the other property of the Guild, and in 1550 they were purchased by the Corporation. Needless perhaps to say, they have been rebuilt more than once, although they have continuously provided for the poor for more than five hundred years.

An interesting antiquarian find was made in a ditch near Poole a few years ago of the seal of John, Duke of Bedford, under whose rule as Regent of France Joan of Arc was burned. The occurrence of the seal on this spot was due, without doubt, to this noble having been Lord of Canford and Poole.

Near the church, a modern building on the site of an older one, is a small gateway which may possibly have been a water gate, as traces of sea-weed were found clinging to it when the adjacent soil was excavated.

Older than any other buildings in Poole are the so-called "Town Cellars", referred to variously in the town's remarkable collection of records as the "Great Cellar", the "King's Hall", and the "Woolhouse". The original purpose of the building has not yet been definitely determined. It is largely of fourteenth-century date, and its doorways and windows have a decidedly ecclesiastical appearance. At the same time there is no evidence whatever that it ever formed part of a monastic foundation, or was ever built for religious purposes. The old battered [Pg 38] building was the scene of at least one fierce fight, when a combined French and Spanish fleet attacked the town to revenge themselves on the dreaded buccaneer, Harry Paye, or Page, who had been raiding the shores of France and Spain. When the hostile fleets entered Poole Harbour early one morning five hundred years ago, the town was taken by surprise. The intrepid "Arripay", as his enemies rendered the name, was absent on one of his expeditions, but his place was worthily taken by his brother, who was killed in the fighting. The Town Cellars were full of stores and munitions of war, and when the building had been captured and set on fire, the townsmen retired, while the victorious Spaniards, who had been reinforced by the French after a first repulse, returned with a few prisoners to their ships, and sailed out of the harbour, having given the mariners of Poole the greatest drubbing they have ever received in the long history of the place.

POOLE HARBOUR FROM CONSTITUTIONAL HILL

Near Poole is Canford Manor, the seat of Lord Wimborne and the "Chene Manor" of the Wessex novels. There was a house here in very early times, and in the sixteenth year of his reign King John, by letter-close, informed Ralph de Parco, the keeper of his wines at Southampton, that it was his pleasure that three tuns "of our wines, of the best sort that is in your custody", should be sent to Canford. In [Pg 39] the fifth year of Henry III the King addressed the following letter to Peter de Mauley: —

"You are to know that we have given to our beloved uncle, William, Earl of Sarum, eighty chevrons (cheverons) in our forest of Blakmore, for the rebuilding of his houses (*ad domos*) at Caneford. Tested at Westminster, 28th July."

The present house occupies the site of the old mansion of the Longspées and Montacutes, Earls of Salisbury, of which the kitchen remains, with two enormous fireplaces, and curious chimney shafts. The greater part of the old mansion was pulled down in 1765, and the house which was then erected became, for a short time, the home of a society of Teresan nuns from Belgium. In 1826 it was again rebuilt by Blore, and in 1848 Sir John Guest employed Sir Charles Barry to make many additions, including the tower, great hall and gallery, leaving, however, the dining-room and the whole of the south front as Blore had designed them. A new wing containing billiard and smoking rooms was added so recently as 1887.

Lady Charlotte Guest, mother of the late Lord Wimborne, was a distinguished Welsh scholar, whose translation of the *Mabinogion* gave an extraordinary impulse to the study of Celtic literature and folk-lore in England. She was twice married, [Pg 40] her first husband being Sir J. J. Guest, and her second Mr. Schreiber, member of Parliament for Poole.

In addition to a great literary talent Lady Charlotte had a considerable love for the more mechanical side of the bookmaker's art, and for many years Canford could boast of a printing press. In the year

1862 serious attention was turned to the production of beautiful and artistic printing. Although Lady Charlotte was the prime mover in this venture, she received valuable assistance from her son (Lord Wimborne), Miss Enid Guest, and other members of the family. It is thought that the first book printed here was *Golconda*, the work of a former tutor to the family. The most important books produced at this amateur press were Tennyson's *The Window*, and *The Victim*, both printed in 1867. One of the Miss Guests had met Tennyson while staying at Freshwater, and the poet sent these MSS. to Canford in order that they might be printed. On the title page of *The Victim* there is a woodcut of Canford Manor. A copy of this book was recently in the market. It contained an autograph inscription by the late Mr. Montague Guest to William Barnes, the Dorset poet. Only two other copies have changed hands since 1887, and these Canford press publications are eagerly [Pg 41] sought by collectors. So long ago as 1896 a copy of *The Victim* realized £75 at the sale of the Crampton Library.

The ancient town of Wimborne, with its glorious minster, is very easily reached both from Poole and from Bournemouth. The town stands in a fertile district which was once occupied by the Roman legions, but the chief glory of the place is its magnificent church with its numerous tombs and monuments. Here are the last resting-places of such famous families as the Courtenays, the Beauforts, and the Uvedales, and here also lie the two daughters of Daniel Defoe, who joined Monmouth's Rebellion at Lyme Regis. In the south choir aisle is the tomb of Antony Etricke, before whom the Duke of Monmouth was taken after his flight from Sedgemoor. The chained library, near the vestry, consists chiefly of books left by William Stone, Principal of New Inn Hall, Oxford, who was a native of the town. In 871 King Ethelred I died of wounds received in a battle against the Danes near Wimborne. He was buried in the minster, where he is commemorated by a fifteenth-century brass, this being the only memorial of the kind that we have of an English monarch.

One cannot wander in these quiet old streets that surround the minster without recalling to memory [Pg 42] the nuns of Wimborne, who settled here about the year 705, and over whom Cuthberga, Queen of Northumbria, and sister of Ina, King of the West Saxons, presided as first abbess. It was with the nuns of Wimborne that St.

Boniface, a native of Crediton, in Devon, contracted those friendships that cast so interesting a light on the character of the great apostle of Germany.

In addition to its minster church, Wimborne has a very old building in St. Margaret's Hospital, founded originally for the relief of lepers. The chapel joins one of the tenements of the almsfolk, and here comes one of the minster clergy every Thursday to conduct divine service. Near a doorway in the north wall is an excellent outside water stoup in a perfect state of preservation.

Comparatively few visitors to Bournemouth and Poole are aware to how large an extent the culture of lavender for commercial purposes is carried on at Broadstone, near Poole. Although it is only during comparatively recent years that the cultivation of lavender in this country has been sufficiently extensive to raise it to the dignity of a recognized industry, dried lavender flowers have been used as a perfume from the days of the Romans, who named the flower *lavandula,* from the use to which it was applied by them in scenting the water for the bath. It is not [Pg 43] known for certain when the lavender plant was brought into England. Shakespeare, in the *Winter's Tale*, puts these words into the mouth of Perdita:

> "Here's flowers for you;
> Hot lavender, mint, savory, marjoram;
> The marigold, that goes to bed with the sun,
> And with him rises weeping: these are flowers of
> Middle summer".

The Bard of Avon laid his scene in Bohemia; but the context makes it evident that the plants named were such as were growing in an English cottager's garden in the reign of Queen Elizabeth.

Broadstone was the spot chosen by Messrs. Rivers Hill and Company for the purpose of growing lavender for their perfume distilleries. It is an ideal spot, where a large tract of heather land, on a portion of Lord Wimborne's estate, rises in a series of undulations from Poole Harbour. Although it is quite a new industry for Dorset, it has already proved of great value in finding constant employment, and an employment as healthy as it is constant, for a large number of men and women. Unfortunately, perhaps, it is an industry which demands peculiar climatic conditions to render it commercially profitable. A close proximity to the sea, and an abundance of sunshine, give an aroma to the oil extracted from the flowers that is lacking when lavender is grown inland.

[Pg 44]

The farm has its own distillery, where the oil essences are extracted and tested. The lavender is planted during the winter months, and two crops are harvested—the first in June or July, and the second in August or September. The reaping is done by men, and the flowers are packed into mats of about half a hundredweight each.

The fields are not entirely given over to the cultivation of lavender, for peppermint, sweet balm, rosemary, elder, and the sweet-scented violets are also grown here. In addition to the people occupied in the fields a large number of women and girls are employed to weave the wicker coverings for the bottles of scent, forwarded from this Dorset flower farm to all parts of the world.

CHRISTCHURCH

The ancient borough of Christchurch, five miles from Bournemouth, spreads itself over a mile of street on a promontory washed on one side by the Dorset Stour, and on the other by the Wiltshire Avon. Just below the town the two rivers unite, and make their way through mud-banks to the English Channel. The town itself is not devoid of interest, although the great attraction of the place is the old Priory church, one [Pg 45] of the finest churches of non-cathedral rank in the country, both with regard to its size, and its value to students of architecture.

Christchurch was once included in the New Forest, the boundaries of which "ran from Hurst along the seashore to Christchurch bridge, as the sea flows, thence as the Avon extends as far as the bridge of Forthingbrugge" (Fordingbridge). Its inclusion in the New Forest probably accounts for the great number of Kings who visited it after the Norman Conquest, although King Ethelwold was here so early as 901, long before the New Forest was thought of. King John had a great liking for this part of the country, where the New Forest, Cranborne Chase, and the Royal Warren of Purbeck made up a hunting-ground of enormous extent. King John was frequently at Christchurch, which was also visited by Edwards I, II, and III, by the seventh and eighth Henrys, and by Edward VI, the last of whom, we are told by Fuller, passed through "the little town in the forest". With such a wealth of royal visitors it is fitting that the principal hotel in the town should be called the "King's Arms". One of the members of Parliament for the borough was the eccentric Antony Etricke, the Recorder of Poole, before whom the Duke of Monmouth was taken after his capture following the defeat at Sedgemoor. The unfortunate prince was found on [Pg 46] Shag's Heath, near Horton, in a field since called "Monmouth's Close".

An interesting reference to the place which has been missed by all the town's historians, including that indefatigable antiquary, Walcott, occurs in "The Note-Book of Tristram Risdon", an early seventeenth-century manuscript preserved in the Library of the Dean and Chapter of Exeter. The entry is as follows: —

"Baldwyn de Ridvers, the fifth, was Erl of Devonshire after the death of Baldwyn his father, which died 29 of Henry III. This Baldwyn had issue John, which lived not long, by meanes whereof the name of Ridvers failed, and th'erldom came unto Isabell sister of the last Baldwyn, which was maried unto William de Fortibus, Erl of Albemarle. This Lady died without issue. Neere about her death shee sold th'ile of Weight, and her mannor of Christchurch unto King Edward I for six thowsand mark, payd by the hands of Sir Gilbert Knovile, William de Stanes, and Geffrey Hecham, the King's Receivers."

Going by the road the town is entered on the north side, at a spot called Bargates, where there was once a movable barrier or gate. Eggheite (i.e. the marshy island), the old name of a suburb of the town, gave the appellation to an extensive Hundred in Domesday. Baldwin de Redvers mentions the bridge of Eggheite. Among the Corporation records are three indulgences remitting forty days of penance granted at Donuhefd by Simon, Archbishop of Canterbury, July 1331, to all who contributed to the building or repair of the bridge of Christchurch de Twyneham; by Gervase, Bishop [Pg 47] of Bangor, in 1367; and by Geoffrey, Archbishop of Damascus, 6th December, 1373. These indulgences are interesting as showing the importance attached to keeping the town's bridges in good repair.

CHRISTCHURCH PRIORY FROM WICK FERRY

This is one of the finest churches of non-Cathedral rank in the country, both with regard to size and its value to students of architecture. It is larger than many a Cathedral.

On 28th January, 1855, Sir Edmund Lyons, afterwards "Lord Lyons of Christchurch", received a public welcome in the town, on his return from his brilliant action before Sebastopol. At Mudeford, near by, lived William Steward Rose, to whom Sir Walter Scott paid occasional visits. Scott is said to have corrected the proofs of "Marmion" while at Mudeford, where, in 1816, Coleridge was staying.

The town once had a leper hospital in Barrack Street, dedicated to St. Mary Magdalen, but all traces of it have disappeared.

The views around the town, especially perhaps that from the top of the church tower, are very extensive, from the New Forest on the east to the hills of Purbeck and Swanage on the west, while the view seawards includes the sweeping curve of Christchurch Bay, the English Channel, and the Isle of Wight. The conspicuous eminence seen on the west of the river is St. Catherine's Hill, where the monks first began to build their Priory, and on it some traces of a small chapel have been found. Hengistbury Head is a wild and deserted spot, with remains of an ancient fosse cut between the Stour and the sea, possibly for [Pg 48] defensive purposes, as there is a rampart on each side of the entrenchment, to which there are three entrances.

At the end of the long High Street stands the Priory church, with examples to show of each definite period of our national ecclesiastical architecture, from an early Norman crypt to Renaissance chantries. The extreme length of the church is 311 feet, it being in this respect of greater length than the cathedrals of Rochester, Oxford, Bristol, Exeter, Carlisle, Ripon, and Southwell.

So vast a building naturally costs a large sum of money every year to keep in repair, and in this respect the parishioners of the ancient borough owe much to Bournemouth, whose visitors, by their fees, provide more than sufficient funds for this purpose. The wonderful purity of the air has been a great factor in preserving the crispness of the masonry, and in keeping the mouldings and carvings almost as sharp in profile as when they were first cut by the mediæval masons.

The out-of-the-way position of the Priory no doubt accounts for the slight and fragmentary references to it in early chronicles, the only old writer of note to mention it being Knyghton (*temp.* Richard II), who speaks of it as "the Priory of Twynham, which is now called Christchurch". Even Camden, many years later, merely says that "Christchurch had a castle and church founded in the time of the Saxons". It [Pg 49] is mentioned in the Domesday Survey, when its value was put at £8 yearly, an increase of two pounds since the days of Edward the Confessor. The Cartulary of the Priory is in the British Museum, but it contains no notes of architectural interest.

According to tradition the first builders began to erect a church on St. Catherine's Hill, but by some miraculous agency the stones were removed every night, and deposited on the promontory between the two rivers, at a spot which became known by the Saxon name of Tweoxneham, or Twynham. The site for the church having been divinely revealed, the monks began to build on the sacred spot; but even then there was no cessation of supernatural intervention. Every day a strange workman came and toiled; but he never took any food to sustain him, and never demanded any wages. Once, when a rafter was too short for its allotted place, the stranger stretched it to the required length with his hands, and this miraculous beam is still to be seen within the church. When at last the building was finished, and the workmen were gathered together to see the fruits of their labour receive the episcopal consecration, the strange workman was nowhere to be found. The monks came to the conclusion that He was none other than Christ Himself, and the church which owed so much to His miraculous help became known as [Pg 50] Christchurch, or Christchurch Twynham, although it had been officially dedicated to the Holy Trinity in the reign of Edward the Confessor, and the title of Christchurch does not appear to have been in general use until the twelfth century.

The early history of the foundation is very obscure. King Aethelstan is said to have founded the first monastery. More certain is it that, in the reign of Edward the Confessor, the church at Twynham was held by Secular Canons, who remained there until 1150, when they were displaced by Augustinians, or Austin Canons. The early church was pulled down by Ralf Flambard, afterwards Bishop of Durham. He was the builder of the fine Norman nave of Christchurch, and the still grander nave of Durham Cathedral. He was Chaplain to William Rufus, and his life was as evil and immoral as his skill in building was great. He died in 1128, and was buried in his great northern cathedral. Much of Flambard's Norman work at Christchurch remains in the triforium, the arcading of the nave, and the transepts. A little later we get the nave clerestory, Early English work, put up soon after the dawn of the thirteenth century, the approximate date also of the nave aisle vaulting, the north porch, and a chapel attached to the north transept. To the fourteenth century belong the massive stone rood-screen, and the reredos. The Perpendicular Lady [Pg 51] Chapel was finished about the close of the thirteenth century, while the fourteenth century gave us the western tower, and most of the choir, although the vaulting was put up much later, as the bosses of the south choir aisle bear the initials W. E., indicating William Eyre, Prior from 1502 to 1520. Last of all in architectural chronology come the chantry of Prior Draper, built in 1529, and that of Margaret, Countess of Salisbury, niece of Edward IV, and mother of the famous Cardinal Pole. She was not destined, however, to lie here, as she was beheaded at the Tower in 1541.

The church now consists of nave, aisles, choir, unaisled transepts, western tower, and Lady Chapel. The cloisters and the domestic buildings have disappeared. It is highly probable that there was once a central tower, an almost invariable accompaniment of a Norman conventual church. There is no documentary evidence relating to a central tower, but the massive piers and arches at the corners of the transepts seem to indicate that provision was made for one, and the representation of a tower of two stages on an old Priory seal, may be either the record of an actual structure, or an intelligent anticipation of a feature that never took an architectural form, although it was contemplated.

In the churchyard are tombstones to the memory of some of the passengers lost in the wreck of the [Pg 52] *Halsewell*, off Durlston Head, on 6th January, 1786. The churchyard is large, and a walk round it allows a view of the whole of the north side of the church. On the south side a modern house and its grounds have displaced the cloisters and the domestic buildings attached to the foundation. Prominent features on the north side are a circular transept stairway, rich in diaper work, the arcading round the transept, the wide windows of the clerestory of the choir, and the upper portion of the Lady Chapel. The fifteenth-century tower is set so far within the nave as to leave two spaces at the ends of the aisles, one used as a vestry, the other as a store-room. In the spandrels of the tower doorway are two shields charged with the arms of the Priory and of the Earls of Salisbury. Above the doorway is a large window, and above this again a niche containing a figure of Christ. The octagonal stair turret is at the north-east angle. The north porch, much restored, is of great size, and its side walls are of nearly the same height as the clerestory of the nave. On the west side is a recess with shafts of Purbeck marble and foliated cusps. Around the wall is a low stone seat, used, it is said, by the parishioners and others who came to see the Prior on business. The roof has some very beautiful groining, much restored in 1862. Above the porch is a lofty room, probably used as the muniment room [Pg 53] of the Priory. Entrance to the church from this porch is through a double doorway of rich Early English work.

PRIORY RUINS, CHRISTCHURCH

An extraordinary epitaph is that on a tombstone near the north porch, which reads as follows: —

> "We were not slayne but raysed, raysed not to life but to be byried twice by men of strife. What rest could the living have when dead had none, agree amongst you heere we ten are one. Hen. Rogers died Aprill 17 1641."

Several attempts have been made to explain the meaning of this epitaph, one to the effect that Oliver Cromwell, while at Christchurch, dug up some lead coffins to make into bullets, replacing the bodies from ten coffins in one grave. This solution is more ingenious than probable, as Cromwell does not appear to have ever been at Christchurch. Moreover, the Great Rebellion did not begin until over fifteen months later than the date on the tombstone. Another and more likely explanation is that the ten were shipwrecked sailors, who were at first buried near the spot where their bodies were washed ashore. The lord of the manor wished to remove the bodies to consecrated ground, and a quarrel ensued between him and Henry Rogers, then Mayor of Christchurch, who objected to their removal. Eventually the lord of the manor had his way, but the Mayor had the bodies placed in one grave, possibly to save the town the expense of ten separate interments.

[Pg 54]

The north aisle was originally Norman, and small round-headed windows still remain to light the triforium. In the angle formed by the aisle and the north wing of the transept stood formerly a two-storied building, the upper part of which communicated by a stair-case with the north aisle, but all this has been destroyed. The north transept is chiefly Norman in character, with a fine arcade of inter-secting arches beneath a billeted string-course. An excellent Norman turret of four stages runs up at the north-east angle, and is richly decorated, the third story being ornamented with a lattice-work of stone in high relief. East of the transept was once an apsidal chapel, similar to that still remaining in the south arm of the transept, but about the end of the thirteenth century this was destroyed and two chapels were built in its place. These contain beautiful examples of plate tracery windows.

Above these chapels is a chamber supposed to have been the tracing room wherein various drawings were prepared. The compartment has a window similar in style to those in the chapels below.

East of the transept is the choir, with a clerestory of four lofty Perpendicular windows of four lights each, with a bold flying buttress between the windows.

The whole of this part of the church is Perpendicular, the choir aisle windows are very low, and the [Pg 55] curvature of the sides of the arches is so slight that they almost appear to be straight lines. The choir roof is flat, and is invisible from the exterior of the church. It is probable that at one time a parapet ran along the top of the clerestory walls, similar to that on the aisle walls, but if so it has disappeared, giving this portion of the choir a somewhat bare appearance. The Lady Chapel is to the east of the choir and presbytery, and contains three large Perpendicular windows on each side; part of the central window on the north side is blocked by an octagonal turret containing a staircase leading to St. Michael's Loft, a large room above the Chapel. The large eastern window of five lights is Perpendicular. The original purpose of the loft above the Chapel is uncertain, and it has been used for a variety of purposes. It was described as "St. Michael's Loft" in 1617, and in 1666 the parishioners petitioned Bishop Morley for permission to use it as a school, describing it as having been "heretofore a chapter-house". The loft is lighted by five two-light windows having square heads and with the lights divided by transoms. The eastern wall has a window of three lights. Very curious are the corbels of the dripstones and the grotesquely carved gargoyles. The south sides of the Lady Chapel and choir correspond very closely with the north. This portion of the church is not so well known as [Pg 56] the north side, as private gardens come close up to the walls.

The Norman apsidal chapel still remains on the eastern side of the south transept. This has a semi-conical roof with chevron tablemoulding beneath it, and clusters of shafts on each side at the spring of the apse. Of the two windows one is Norman and the other Early English. On the northern side of the apse is an Early English sacristy. The south side of the transept was strengthened by three buttresses, and contains a depressed segmental window much smaller than the corresponding window of the north transept. The south side of the nave has, externally, but little interest as compared to the north side, for the cloisters, which originally stood here, have been pulled down. Traces of the cloister roof can still be seen, also a large drain, and an aumbry and cupboard built into the thickness of the wall. There are also the remains of a staircase which probably led to a dormitory at the western end.

In the south wall of the nave are two doors, that at the west used by the canons, and that at the east by the Prior. The latter door is of thirteenth-century date and is distinctly French in character.

In mediæval days the nave was used as the parish church, and had its own high altar, while the choir was reserved for the use of the canons. The nave [Pg 57] is made up of seven noble bays; the lower arcade consists of semicircular arches enriched with the chevron ornament, while the spandrels are filled with hatchet-work carving. The triforium of each bay on both sides consists of two arches supported by a central pillar and enclosed by a semicircular containing arch, with bold mouldings.

The clerestory was built about 1200 by Peter, the third Prior. The present roof is of stucco, added in 1819; the original Norman roof was probably of wood, although springing shafts exist, which seem to indicate that a stone vault was contemplated by the Norman builders. The north aisle retains its original stone vaulting, put up about 1200. This aisle is slightly later than the southern one, which was completed first in order that the cloister might be built. The windows are of plate tracery, and mark the transition between Early English and Decorated. The south aisle is very richly decorated with a fine wall arcade enriched with cable and billet mouldings. The vaulting is of the same date as that in the north aisle, and is also the work of Peter, Prior from 1195 to 1225. In the western bay is the original Norman window, the others being filled with modern tracery of Decorated style. In this aisle is a large aumbry and recess, where the bier and lights used at funerals were stored. There [Pg 58] is also a holy-water stoup in the third bay. At the west end are the remains of the stairway which led to the dormitory. The stairway is built into the wall, which, at this particular spot, is nearly seven feet thick.

Under the north transept is an early Norman apsidal crypt with aumbries in the walls. There is a corresponding crypt in the south wing.

The ritual choir of the canons included the transept crossing as well as one bay of the parish nave, but at a later date the ritual and the new architectural choirs were made to correspond, and the present stone rood-screen was erected. It dates from the time of Edward III. It has a plain base, surmounted with a row of panelled quatrefoils, over which is a string-course with a double tier of canopied niches. The whole screen is massive and of superb workmanship.

The choir is of Perpendicular architecture, lighted by four lofty windows on each side. There is no triforium, its place being occupied with panelling. On each side of the choir are fifteen stalls with quaintly carved misericords.

The presbytery stands on a Norman crypt, and is backed by a stone reredos far exceeding in beauty the somewhat similar screens at Winchester, Southwark, and St. Albans. It is of three stories, with [Pg 59] five compartments in each tier, and represents the genealogy of our Lord. The screen is flanked on the north side by the Salisbury Chapel. In the crypt beneath is the chantry of de Redvers, now walled up to form a family vault for the Earls of Malmesbury, lay rectors of the church.

The Lady Chapel is vaulted like the choir, from which it is an eastern extension, and has a superb reredos dating from the time of Henry VI. The Chapel contains several tombs and monuments, including that of Thomas, Lord West, who bequeathed six thousand marks to maintain a chantry of six priests.

Beneath the tower is the marble monument by Weekes to the memory of the poet Shelley, who was drowned by the capsizing of a boat in the Gulf of Spezzia in 1822. Below the name "Percy Bysshe Shelley" are the following lines from his "Adonais":—

"He has outsoared the shadow of our night;
Envy and calumny and hate and pain,
And that unrest which men miscall delight,
Can touch him not and torture not again:
From the contagion of the world's slow stain
He is secure, and now can never mourn
A heart grown cold, a head grown grey in vain;
Nor, when the spirits' self has ceased to burn,
With sparkless ashes load an unlamented urn".

At the Reformation the domestic buildings were pulled down, and the old Priory church became the [Pg 60] parish church of Christchurch. The last Prior was John Draper II, vicar of Puddletown, Dorset, and titular Bishop of Neapolis. He surrendered the Priory on 28th November, 1539, when he received a pension of £133, 6s. 8d.; and was allowed to retain Somerford Grange during his life. The original document reads: —

> "To John Draper, Bishop of Neapolytan, late prior there (Christchurch), £133, 6s. 8d.; also the manor of Somerford, called the Prior's lodging, parcel of the manor of Somerford, being part of the said late monastery, for term of life of the said bishop without anything yielding or paying thereof."

The other inmates of the monastery also received pensions. The debts owed by the brethren at the Dissolution include such items as: —

> "To John Mille, Recorder of Southampton, for wine and ale had of him, £24, 2s. 8d. William Hawland, of Poole, merchant, for wine, fish, and beer had of him, £8, 13s. 2d. Guillelmus, tailor, of Christchurch, as appeareth by his bill, 26s. Roger Thomas, of Southampton, for a pair of organs, £4."

Heron Court was the Prior's country house, while Somerford and St. Austin's, near Lymington, were granges and lodges belonging to the foundation.

On leaving the Priory a visit should be paid to the ruins of the old Norman Castle, perched on the top of a high mound that commands the town on every side, and the Priory as well. Only fragments of the walls remain of the keep erected here by [Pg 61] Richard de Redvers, who died in 1137, although the castle continued to be held by his descendants until it was granted by Edward III to William de Montacute, Earl of Salisbury, who was appointed Constable, an office he held until 1405. During the tenure by the de Redvers the resident bailiff regulated the tolls, markets, and fairs at his pleasure, and he also fixed the amount of the duties to be levied on merchandise. It was not until the reign of the third Edward that the burgesses were relieved from these uncertain and arbitrary exactions.

PLACE MILL, CHRISTCHURCH

Place Mill was formerly called "The Old Priory Mill" and is mentioned in the Domesday Survey

The east and west walls of the keep remain, ten feet in thickness and about thirty feet in height. The artificial mound on which they are raised is well over twenty feet high.

The masonry of the walls is exceedingly rough and solid, for in the days when they were erected men built for shelter and protection, and not with the idea of providing themselves with beautiful houses to live in. The keep was made a certain height, not as a crowning feature in the landscape, but so that from its top the warder could see for many miles the glitter of a lance, or the dust raised by a troop of horsemen. One of the greatest charms of the rough, solid walls of a Norman castle is that they are so honest and straightforward, and tell their story so plainly.

[Pg 62]

Looking over the town from the Castle mound we realize that Christchurch could correctly be denominated a "moated town", inasmuch as its two rivers encircle it in a loving embrace. Being so cut off by Nature with waterways as to be almost an island, it was obviously a strong position for defence, and a lovely site for a monastery.

A little to the north-east of the Castle, upon a branch of the Avon which formed at once the Castle moat and the Priory mill stream, stands a large portion of one of the few Norman houses left in this country. It is seventy feet long by thirty feet in breadth, with walls of great thickness. It was built about the middle of the thirteenth century, and is said, on slight authority, to have been the Constable's house. The basement story has widely-splayed loopholes in its north and east walls, and retains portions of the old stone staircases which led to the principal room occupying the whole of the upper story. This upper room was lighted by three Norman windows on each side, enriched with the billet, zigzag, and rosette mouldings.

At the north end the arch and shafts remain of a large window decorated with the familiar chevron ornament. Near the centre of the east wall is a fireplace with a very early specimen of a round chimney, which has, however, been restored. In the south gable is [Pg 63] a round window, while a small tower, forming a flank, overhangs the stream which flows through it. The building is much overgrown with ivy and creepers, and it is a matter for regret that no efficient means have been taken to preserve so valuable a specimen of late Norman architecture from slowly crumbling to pieces under the influences of the weather. Traces of the other sides of the Castle moat have been discovered in Church Street, Castle Street, and in the boundary of the churchyard.

A walk along the bank situated between the Avon proper and the stream that flows by the side of the Norman house leads past the Priory and the churchyard to the Quay, the spot where much of the stone for building the Priory was disembarked. Owing to the estuary of the combined rivers being almost choked with mud and weeds there is very little commercial shipping trade carried on at the Quay, which is now mainly the centre of the town's river life during the summer months, for everyone living at Christchurch seems to own a boat of some kind. During the season motor launches ply several times a day between Christchurch and Mudeford, with its reputation for Christchurch salmon.

On the quayside is the old Priory Mill, now called Place Mill, which is mentioned in the Domesday Survey. It stands on the very brink of the river; [Pg 64] its foundations are deep set in the water, and its rugged and buttressed walls are reflected stone by stone in the clear, tremulous mirror. The glancing lights on the bright stream, the wealth of leafy foliage, the sweet cadence of the ripples as they plash against the walls of the Quay, and the beauty of the long reflections—quivering lines of grey, green, and purple—increase the beauty of what is probably the most picturesque corner of the town, while over the tops of the trees peers the grey tower of the ancient Priory church. These three buildings—the Priory, the Castle, and the Mill—sum up the simple history of the place. The Castle for defence, the Priory for prayer, the Mill for bread; and of Christchurch it may be said, both by the historian and the modern sightseer, *haec tria sunt omnia*.